# THE BRITISH EXECUTION

# Stephen Banks

SHIRE PUBLICATIONS

Published in Great Britain in 2013 by Shire Publications Ltd, Midland House, West Way, Botley, Oxford OX2 0PH, United Kingdom.

43-01 21st Street, Suite 220B, Long Island City, NY 11101, USA.

E-mail: shire@shirebooks.co.uk    www.shirebooks.co.uk

© 2013 Stephen Banks.

A CIP catalogue record for this book is available from the British Library.

Shire Library no. 744.    ISBN-13: 978 0 74781 242 5

Stephen Banks has asserted his right under the Copyright, Designs and Patents Act, 1988, to be identified as the author of this book.

Designed by Tony Truscott Designs, Sussex, UK and typeset in Perpetua and Gill Sans.

Printed in China through Worldprint Ltd.

13 14 15 16 17    10 9 8 7 6 5 4 3 2 1

COVER IMAGE
The Irish revolutionary and poet Robert Emmet was executed for treason in Dublin on 20 September 1803.

TITLE PAGE IMAGE
The block, axe and executioner's mask at the Tower of London. (Painting by John Fulleylove in Arthur Poyser, *The Tower of London*, 1908.)

CONTENTS PAGE IMAGE
On a trumped-up accusation by Titus Oates, Edward Coleman is drawn up on a hurdle to Tyburn to be executed for his alleged part in a suspected Popish Plot in 1678: with him is Jack Ketch the executioner. (Woodcut illustration to the *Bagford Ballads*.)

ACKNOWLEDGEMENTS
I would like to thank those who have allowed me to use illustrations, which are acknowledged as follows:

Mary Evans/Library of Congress, page 6; Mary Evans/Grosvenor Prints, page 10; Mary Evans/Glasshouse Images, page 12 (top); Mary Evans/Interfoto/Sammlung Rauch, page 12 (bottom); Interfoto/NG Collection/Mary Evans, page 13 (bottom left); Mary Evans/Peter Higginbotham Collection, page 14 (bottom); Interfoto/Sammlung Rauch/Mary Evans, page 17 (right); Mary Evans/Interfoto, page 30; Mary Evans/Bruce Castle Museum, page 37; Interfoto/Bildarchiv Hansmann/Mary Evans, page 40; Illustrated London News Ltd/Mary Evans, page 48, 61; Mary Evans/The National Archives, page 52.

All other images are courtesy of the Mary Evans Picture Library.

Shire Publications is supporting the Woodland Trust, the UK's leading woodland conservation charity, by funding the dedication of trees.

# CONTENTS

uant la feste fut
paffee, les mefke
wuon qui point
neftoit ammelo

# THE FATAL PERFORMANCE

THIS BOOK concerns itself with capital punishment in Britain from the time of the Tudor kings up until the final execution in 1964. By way of an introduction however, it is useful both to visit earlier periods in British history and to observe that capital punishment was rarely a simple matter of putting a criminal to death quickly and discreetly. Rather it was a performance, held in public until 1868, and one that was designed to convey many messages to those who might see it. Historically, the scaffold was seen as a place of educational opportunity, where one could explain the character of the crime, justify the appointed retribution and hopefully deter further offences.

Execution, then, was theatre, with its own conventions and symbolism, and this has been true since ancient times. Justinian's *Institutes* tells us that when a man in Rome killed his own father, the Romans displayed their horror by sewing him up in a sack with a dog, a cock, a snake and a monkey and hurling him from the Tarpeian Rock. In England, as in other countries, traitors were dragged to their deaths on hurdles to signify that their feet were unworthy of touching the ground. Heretics sent to the stake were forced to wear vestments or hats depicting devils and flames, a reminder that the burning of their body was but a foretaste of the eternal fire that awaited them.

Doubtless, many spectators derived satisfaction from seeing due punishment inflicted. In feudal societies, however, a crime was as much an offence against the monarch as against any individual or community. People were subjects of, and to an extent, the property of, their sovereign, so if one man killed another he deprived the king of the service or value of the deceased. A serious crime could therefore be construed as an act of rebellion. The French philosopher, Michel Foucault, writing of a particularly prolonged execution in France in 1757, argued that the purpose of torture and protracted punishments was to demonstrate that the power of the king was overwhelming and able to defeat any attempt to injure his sovereignty.

In Anglo-Saxon England things were somewhat different. Central power was weak and the kings were concerned to prevent blood feuds among warring

A contemporary
woodcut depicting
the burning of the
Czech religious
reformer Johannes
Hus in 1415.
Note the heretics'
crown depicting
Satan's demons.

families or clans. Capital punishment was inflicted, but there was also a system
of compensation whereby a man who had slain another could pay blood
money to the murdered man's family and so prevent either a feud or a
prosecution. The system seems, however, to have been swept aside with

the Norman invasion of 1066. It is very likely that the number of executions increased under the Normans, not merely because of the disappearance of blood money, but also because of the establishment of Forest Laws. These were designed to preserve game over large swathes of England for the sporting nobility, and poachers were liable to be flayed, mutilated or hanged. The system of compensation was certainly gone by the time that Henry II (1133–89) centralised many aspects of justice and established trial by jury in the royal courts in 1166.

Hanging meant slow asphyxiation. It was only in the latter part of the nineteenth century that British hangmen became able to calculate drops and to position the noose in such as way as to break the neck and cause almost instant death. Even then, as we shall see, mistakes were made. In the earlier period a 'turning off' often meant little more than a rope being thrown around a tree while the culprit stood up in a cart with the noose around his neck. The cart drove off and the felon was left suspended a few feet from the ground. Relatives might rush forward to tug upon the feet of the swinging felon in order to speed his demise and it is in this context that the beheading of well-born offenders should be understood as having evolved as a merciful concession to their gentility.

A hanging in Anglo-Saxon England. Death came by slow strangulation. (Reproduction of a manuscript in Strutt's *Antiquities* (1793), Vol. I, Plate XV.)

Traitors, no matter how highly born, could expect more exemplary punishment. High and petty treason were defined in the Treason Act of 1351, but terrible penalties were already being imposed. Jean Froissart's *Chronicles* gives a detailed account of the sentence imposed in 1326 upon Hugh Despenser the Younger, a one-time favourite of Edward II. After his faction was defeated by Queen Isabella, Hugh was dragged by horses to a high gallows and suspended for a time. However, before he could expire he was cut down and tied to a ladder. His genitals were then cut off and thrown into a fire and his intestines were slowly pulled out from his body and burnt. According to Froissart, he emitted one long hideous shriek before his heart was finally cut out, his body quartered and beheaded and the pieces exhibited on the gates of London.

As troubled as England was throughout the High Middle Ages (c. 1000–1300) and into the Late Middle Ages (c. 1300–1500), executioners of these times were little troubled either by heretics or witches. Heresy did not appear in England until the time of the theologian John Wycliffe (c. 1330–84). Wycliffe's followers, a somewhat disparate group known as the Lollards, have been connected, albeit not without some difficulty, with the Protestants of the later Reformation. Lollardy, among the middling classes, penetrated Oxford University and influenced the royal court for a time. Henry IV

(1367–1413) and Henry V (1386–1422) both determined to stamp it out. A statute in 1401, *De Heretico Comburendo* (2 Hen.4 c.15), authorised the burning of heretics, and one of the most important Lollards to suffer this fate was Sir John Oldcastle. In 1417, he was hung in chains over a fire at St Giles Fields in London. Lollardy did not entirely disappear, however, and throughout the fifteenth century there were occasional burnings.

Of witchcraft however, there was little sign. Witchcraft is not a particularly ancient offence in the British Isles. Indeed, the very early church had denied that there could be such a thing as witchcraft at all. It was not a felony in royal courts, although there had been some prosecutions in ecclesiastical courts. However, from the fourteenth century onwards a fear of witches spread through the continent, much enhanced in 1486 by the publication of Heinrich Kramer and James Sprenger's *Malleus Maleficarum*, the 'Hammer of Witches.' However, when Henry VII (1457–1509) defeated Richard III at the battle of Bosworth Field in 1485, he inherited a kingdom that was, for the most part, barely troubled by religious schism and one that had resisted the witchcraft hysteria sweeping the continent. Henry, careful to cement his power, did little to alter this state of affairs. However, when his son succeeded to the throne in 1509 things began to change.

Opposite: The Tower of London in 1415, as depicted in a Flemish illustration to the poems of the duc D'Orleans, who was held there after being taken captive at Agincourt. (1500 British Museum series III. I.)

Sir John Oldcastle is roasted in chains in 1417. (Engraving by T. Smith in Fox's *The Primitive Martyrs*, 1563.)

ENGRAVED for the PRIMITIVE MARTYRS.

The Cruel Martyrdom of S. John Oldcastle LORD COBHAM.

T. Smith delin et sculp.

No. 10. Red Lion Street, Clerkenwell.

Published as the Act directs for H.Tripp, Pater-noster-Row.

# PUNISHING THE BRITISH

IN VIEW OF WHAT WAS TO FOLLOW, it is one of the great ironies of history that Henry VIII (1491–1547) was granted the title of 'Defender of the Faith' by Pope Leo X. This was in recognition of his publication of a book, *Assertio Septem Sacramentorum*, acknowledging the supremacy of the Pope and the sanctity of marriage. Henry has earned his place as one of the most ruthless of all English monarchs. In 1532, he reintroduced the horrific punishment of boiling for poisoners, after a cook, Richard Rice, attempted to poison the Bishop of Rochester's household. Two people died and Rice was slowly plunged up and down into a cauldron of boiling water until he expired. Boiling thereafter was rarely employed, although a female poisoner was executed in this way in 1542.

It is doubtful that Henry was much motivated by concern for the Bishop of Rochester, John Fisher. Henry had already decided to break with Rome so that he could marry Anne Boleyn and Fisher was one of his most prominent opponents. Thomas Cranmer, Archbishop of Canterbury, was more compliant. He declared that Henry's previous marriage to Catherine of Aragon was null and void and Henry married Anne on 25 January 1533. Thus began a period of English history in which both Protestants and Catholics freely employed the charges of both treason and heresy against their opponents. One of the early victims was Fisher, attainted for treason for refusing to take the oath acknowledging Henry as Supreme Head of the Church of England. Although sentenced to be hanged, drawn and quartered, Henry commuted the sentence to beheading, probably for fear of arousing popular sympathy for Fisher. The sentence was carried out on Tower Hill on 22 June 1535, Fisher meeting his death calmly. The body was abandoned naked on the scaffold but eventually it was laid to rest in the churchyard of All Hallows-by-the-Tower. The head adorned a pole on London Bridge until it was thrown into the Thames. The head of Thomas More, beheaded on 6 July, took Fisher's place on display.

Henry, of course, was not above employing charges of treason against unsatisfactory wives and Anne did not last long. She was aged about thirty-two

Opposite:
The execution of the Earl of Derby in the marketplace of Bolton in 1651 in revenge for his sacking of the town.

Portrait of Henry
VIII (1491–1547)
at the age of 49,
painted in 1540
by Hans Holbein
theYounger. Henry
reintroduced
boiling as
the penalty
for poisoners.

when she married him, rather old by the standards of the time. Crowned Queen on 1 June 1533, she gave birth to the future Elizabeth I on 7 September. Her rapid downfall, however, was occasioned by a number of miscarriages, notably that of a male child in 1536. Henry despaired of an heir by Anne and she was soon accused of adultery, incest and high treason. Although she and her alleged lovers were executed, the evidence against them was actually very slight. It mostly depended upon the confession, obtained under torture, of Mark Smeaton, her musician. She died on 19 May 1536 on a scaffold erected on the White Tower, part of the Tower of London, under the sword of an executioner specially brought from France. According to Anthony Kingston, the Constable of the Tower, on the final day she fretted that the time of her death had not been set until midday: 'I am very sorry therefore, for I thought to be dead by this time and past my pain'. The *Annals of John Stow* reported her final words:

John Fisher, Bishop
of Rochester, is
beheaded in 1535
for opposing the
break with Rome.
(Review of *Fox's
Book of Martyrs* by
William Andrews,
1826.)

'I beseech Jesu save my Sovereign and master the King, the most goodliest, and gentlest Prince that is, and long to reign over you', which words she spake with a smiling countenance: which done, she kneeled down on both her knees, and said, 'To Jesu Christ I commend my soul' and with that word suddenly the hangman of Calais smote off her head at one stroke with a sword.

Catherine Howard, Henry's fifth wife, proved similarly unsatisfactory and lasted only two years before she lost her head in the Tower on 13 February 1542. She too was convicted of adultery and attainted for treason. The evidence against her was perhaps somewhat stronger and she may well have had an affair with a courtier, Thomas Culpeper, and her personal secretary Francis Dereham. She was dispatched with the axe.

The next victim, Lady Jane Grey, was, however, entirely innocent. It was her misfortune to be the great-granddaughter of Henry VII. When Henry VIII died in 1547, his only son Edward VI (1537–53) succeeded. Edward was a sickly child. The next in line to the throne was Mary (1516–58), the Catholic daughter of Henry and Catherine of Aragon. To prevent Mary's succession a Protestant alliance was formed by marrying Jane, daughter of the Duke of Suffolk, to Guildford Dudley, the son of the Duke of Northumberland. As Edward lay dying, he was induced to make a will declaring Jane his successor. She was proclaimed Queen on 10 July 1553, but reigned for only nine days. Crucially, Mary was not taken into custody and so was able to rally the country around her. Sensing the way things were going, the Privy Council promptly switched sides and imprisoned Jane in

Far left: Anne Boleyn, Henry VIII's second and ill-fated wife, was convicted of adultery, incest and treason and executed in 1536. (Anonymous sixteenth-century painting.)

Left: Catherine Howard, the fifth wife of Henry VIII, who was beheaded in 1542. (Engraving by Cheesman, c. 1800, after a drawing by Holbein.)

the Tower. At first she, her husband and her father were spared. However, an abortive Protestant rebellion led by Sir Thomas Wyatt convinced Mary that the three were too dangerous to be allowed to live. On 12 February 1554, Guildford was beheaded on Tower Hill and Jane suffered a similar fate in more private circumstances on Tower Green inside the Tower itself. Her father, the Duke of Suffolk, was beheaded on 23 February. Jane, little more than a pawn in the political game, was only sixteen or seventeen at the time of her death.

The final noble lady under consideration here was made of entirely different stuff. Mary, (1542–87) the queen regnant of Scotland and one-time wife of Francis II of France, was implicated, along with her third husband the Earl of Bothwell, in the suspicious death of Henry Darnley, her second husband. Following an uprising against her she fled to England in 1568, apparently hoping that Elizabeth I (1533–1603) would support her claim to the Scottish throne. The problem was that Mary was both a Catholic and the grand-daughter of Margaret Tudor, the sister of Henry VIII. Since Henry's marriage to Anne Boleyn was regarded by many Catholics as illegitimate,

The Traitor's Gate
seen from inside
the Tower.
(John Fulleylove
*The Tower of
London*, 1908.)

The execution of Sir Thomas Wyatt, leader of a Protestant uprising against Mary I. The revolt failed and led, abeit indirectly, to the death of Lady Jane Grey.

Lady Jane Grey was executed at the Tower of London in February 1554. Her husband had already been despatched on the same day on Tower Hill. (Reproduction of an1833 painting by Paul Delaroche.)

in their eyes Mary was the rightful Queen of England. Elizabeth therefore shut Mary up in fairly comfortable captivity for eighteen years, during which time they never met. A number of Catholic plots were hatched to put Mary on the throne, although it is unclear how much she herself knew about them.

Mary's fate was sealed in 1586 when Sir Antony Babington launched a new conspiracy and, in secret correspondence, Mary seemed to agree to the assassination of Elizabeth. The correspondence was intercepted by Elizabeth's minister, Sir Francis Walsingham, and Mary was convicted of treason and executed at Fotheringhay Castle on 8 February 1587. She ascended the steps of the scaffold erected in the great hall and disrobed to reveal a bodice and petticoat of dark red. Robert Wynkfielde reported that her last words were, 'Into thy hands, O Lord, I commend my spirit'. Then one of the executioners held her hand and:

Mary, Queen of Scots (1542–87), was implicated in the murder of her second husband and condemned for her role in the Babington Plot.

She endured two strokes of the other executioner with an axe, she making very small noise or none at all, and not stirring any part of her from the place where she lay: and so the executioner cut off her head, saving one little gristle, which being cut asunder, he lift up her head to the view of all the assembly and bade *God save the Queen* ... Her lips stirred up and down a quarter of an hour after her head was cut off.

Wynkefielde also reported that when Mary's body was being stripped a lap dog was discovered hiding under her petticoats, which refused to leave her side.

When her son James IV of Scotland (1566–1625) became James I of England, he had her remains interred at Westminster Abbey.

Mary, Queen of Scots, is executed at Fotheringay Castle on 8 February 1587. It was said her lips moved up and down for fifteen minutes after her head was struck off. (From *Teatrum crudelitatum*, 1588.)

It hardly seems appropriate to describe these unfortunates as 'lucky' but they were in the respect that they were spared the fate of lesser mortals convicted under the Treason Act. The sentence imposed on Guy Fawkes for his attempt to blow up Parliament and assassinate James I in 1605 was both deeply symbolic and fearful. He was:

> To be drawn to the place of Execution from his Prison, as being not worthy any more to tread upon the Face of the Earth whereof he was made ... he must be drawn with his Head declining downward, and lying so near the Ground as may be, being thought unfit to take benefit of the common Air. For which Cause also he shall be strangled, being hanged up by the Neck between Heaven and Earth, as deemed unworthy of both, or either ... he is to be cut down alive, and to have his Privy Parts cut off and burnt before his Face, as being unworthily begotten, and unfit to leave any Generation after him. His Bowels and inlay'd Parts taken out and burnt, who inwardly had conceived and harboured in his heart such horrible Treason. After, to have his Head cut off, which had imagined the Mischief. And lastly, his Body to be quartered, and the Quarters set up in some high and eminent Place, to the View and Detestation of Men, and to become a Prey for the Fowls of the Air.

Fawkes had named seven fellow conspirators under torture, and four were executed in St Paul's Churchyard on 30 January 1606.

Guy Fawkes prior to his arrest for the Gunpowder Plot. (A contempory engraving, later coloured.)

Concilivm Septem Nobilivm Anglorvm Conivrantivm in Necem Jacobi I.
Magnæ Britanniæ Regis, Totivsq Anglici Convocati Parliementi.
1. Bates - 2. Robert Winter - 3. Christopher Wright - 4. John Wright - 5. Thomas Percy - 6. Guido Fawkes - 7. Robert Catesby - 8. Thomas Winter.

The conspirators in the Gunpowder Plot of 1605. Guy Fawkes is no. 6.

17

The record of the examination of Guy Fawkes in 1606. The record is signed by Guido Fawkes, Sir John Popham, Sir Edward Coke and Mr W. Wood (clerk) but after torture the signature of Fawkes has become a mere scrawl.

The following day, Fawkes was reserved for the very last but according to the *Weekly News* of 31 January 1606, he escaped the full horror of disembowelling and quartering by breaking his neck in a jump from the scaffold. In the struggle over religious orthodoxy, whichever side was in the ascendancy sentenced their opponents to this appalling fate. Henry VIII may perhaps be said to have begun it when he imposed this sentence upon the monk Richard Reynolds, who had been the very first to refuse to take the Oath of Supremacy. He and three others were hanged, drawn and quartered at Tyburn in London on 4 May 1535. Reynolds and thirty-nine other Catholics who had been executed for treason between 1535 and 1679 were canonised by the Pope in 1970.

The conspirators in the Gunpowder Plot are hanged, drawn and then quartered. Fawkes escaped the full horror of the punishment by leaping from the gallows and breaking his neck. (An engraving by Hoogenborgh, 1606.)

It was nine Protestants, however, who suffered this fate in October 1660, after the Restoration and the conclusion of the English Civil Wars. During the conflict, atrocities were perpetrated by both sides. The most illustrious victim was, of course, Charles I himself. Charles was beheaded on 30 January 1649, and could have avoided execution had he renounced his belief in the divine right of kings. He had refused to do so and at his trial in Westminster Hall on 20 January 1649 had demanded, 'I would know by what power I am called

hither. I would know by what authority, I mean lawful'. He refused to plead and his last words upon the scaffold set up outside the Palace of Whitehall were, 'I am a martyr of the people'.

St Richard Reynolds, scholar and Catholic martyr, who refused to take the Oath of Supremacy.

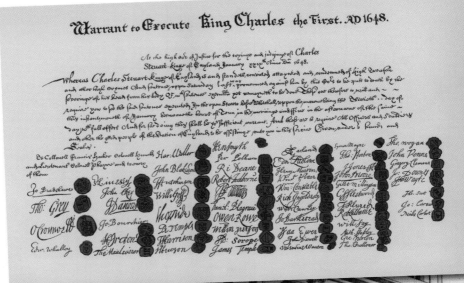

Above:
The warrant
for the execution
of Charles I.

Right:
The scaffold
erected in
Whitehall in 1649.
(Unknown artist,
eighteenth
century.)

Other royalists followed, such as James Stanley, 7th Earl of Derby, who had allegedly slaughtered up to 1,600 inhabitants of Bolton after the storming of the town in May 1644. Eventually captured in Chester, he was taken to the town's Market Cross and beheaded there on 15 October 1651 (see page 10).

With the restoration of Charles II (1630–85) in 1660, the boot was on the other foot. Royalists were determined to make an example of the regicides who had signed Charles I's execution warrant, or those who had assisted in carrying it out. Of those still alive, some fled to America or the continent. But nine met a

K. Charles I. murthered. Pl. 31.

Into thine hands I comit my Spirit: thou haſt redeemed me O Lord God of truth v. 5. For I have heard the ſlander of many while they took counſel together againſt me, to take away my life. v. 13

Above: Charles prepares to kneel before the executioner. His last words were 'I am a martyr of the people.' (Popular contemporary print.)

James Stanley, the Royalist Earl of Derby, who massacred 1,600 civilians at the siege of Bolton in 1644. (Engraving by an unnamed artist after Antony van Dijk in John Thane's *British Autography*, 1794, Vol. II)

horrible end, including John Cook, the distinguished lawyer who had prosecuted Charles I, and the doughty Major General Thomas Harrison. As Harrison was being prepared for disembowelling, he managed to strike the executioner, which provoked, as he surely hoped, his swift beheading. Samuel Pepys witnessed Harrison's execution at Charing Cross on 13 October and described him as 'looking as cheerfully as any man could do in that condition'.

The degree of suffering endured depended very much upon the length of time that the offender was allowed to hang before being cut down for evisceration. Anthony Babington was said to have suffered so severely that even the hardened Tudor crowd protested. Further malefactors suffered the fate of the regicides: notably in 1678, an alleged Catholic conspiracy against James II, the 'Popish Plot', led to the hanging, drawing and quartering of William Staley, who had the dubious distinction of being the last person whose head was displayed on London Bridge. The plot was in fact completely fabricated, but managed also to claim the life of Oliver Plunket, Archbishop of Armagh, the last Catholic priest to be martyred at Tyburn in July 1681.

A contemporary woodcut of the dismemberment of the regicides in 1660.

Things began to change during the eighteenth century, when victims were generally hanged until they were dead before being quartered. This was the case with those Jacobites, such as Lord Lovat, executed for their part in the 1745 rebellion. After 1795, quartering was remitted, so that when Robert Emmett was executed for high treason in Dublin on 20 September 1803, he was hanged and beheaded but not dismembered. In the same year,

Colonel Despard was executed in London. Although drawn on a hurdle around a prison yard in token of the old punishment, he too suffered the same fate as Emmett. Decapitation was abolished in 1870 when the penalty for treason became hanging alone.

Women, it should be pointed out, were never drawn and quartered. For reasons of decency, they were burnt for both high and petty treason. Petty treason involved two types of offences: coining or clipping, or the murder of one's husband. The first consisted of making counterfeit coins or else shaving off precious metal from the genuine article. Murder of one's husband was particularly heinous since it involved rebelling against the natural order of authority in the household as ordained by God. The culprit was tied to a stake with kindling placed all around. If the fire was large and fierce, carbon monoxide poisoning would probably kill the victim before she burned: small, slow fires were much worse. By the eighteenth century, the normal practice was to strangle the culprit before the fire reached her.

The very last burning alive was that of Catherine Hayes on 9 May 1726. She had conspired with two lovers to murder her husband. One account asserts that the executioner delayed too long before trying to strangle her and was forced by the flames to let go of the rope. Others have suggested that she was deliberately left to suffer. Between 1735 and 1789 at least thirty-two women were strangled and burnt in England, the very last occurring in a

Above:
Irish Catholic Oliver Plunket, the Archbishop of Armagh and primate of Ireland, was falsely accused of conspiracy by Titus Oates and hanged, disembowelled and quartered in London. (Unnamed artist.)

Far left: Simon Fraser, Lord Lovat, (1667–1747), a famous Jacobite known as the 'Fox of the North'. (From a painting by William Hogarth.)

Left:
Edward Despard, an Irish soldier who served with distinction in central America, here depicted making a final speech from the scaffold in 1803. (Granger's New Wonderful Museum, 1803.)

street near Newgate on 18 March 1789. Catherine Murphy was forced to stand on a platform alongside a stake driven into the highway, a noose was placed around her neck and she was throttled as the platform was removed. Her body was then burnt on the spot and traffic passed over the ashes.

The burning of both men and women for heresy has become particularly associated in English history with Queen Mary's attempt in the 1550s to restore the Roman Church, but in fact there had been occasional burnings since the passing of the law of *De Heretico Comburendo* by Parliament in 1401, which allowed the burning of heretics. Ironically, some of these were of Protestant reformers under Henry VIII, notably Thomas Hitton, burnt at Maidstone on 23 February 1530. During Mary's reign, however, at least 287 Protestants met their death this way, including the three so-called 'Oxford Martyrs'. Two of them, Hugh Latimer, the former Bishop of Worcester, and Nicholas Ridley, former Bishop of London, were burnt on 16 October 1555 outside Balliol College Oxford, in what is now Broad Street. Ridley had supported Lady Jane Grey and had denounced Mary as illegitimate. Both men refused to recant their faith and it is said that Ridley suffered horribly. Too much wood had been placed on the fire which burnt very slowly, consuming his lower half before he actually expired. Sadly, the story in the second edition of John Foxe's *Acts and Monuments* that Latimer had said to Ridley at the stake, 'Be of good comfort, and play the man, Master Ridley; we shall this day light such a candle, by God's grace, in England, as I trust shall never be put out', cannot be substantiated.

Mary Tudor (1516–58). Known as 'Bloody Mary', it is doubtful that her methods were more ruthless than those of her predecessors or successors. (Unattributed engraving.)

Watching the burnings, under guard, was Thomas Cranmer, the Archbishop of Canterbury, who is perhaps most remembered as the compiler of the first two editions of the *Book of Common Prayer*. Under Mary, Cranmer was imprisoned for two years, and during that time recanted his faith several times. Mary, however, was determined to proceed with his execution. His final recantation was to have been in public at the University Church in Oxford and he wrote out and submitted a speech in advance. During the course of it however, he broke away from the script suddenly, declaring 'And as for the Pope, I refuse him, as Christ's enemy, and Antichrist with all his false doctrine.' He was dragged from the pulpit and burnt upon the same spot as Ridley and Latimer on 21 March 1556. An anonymous eye-witness account reports that:

The burning of bishops Ridley and Latimer for heresy outside Balliol College in Oxford on 16 October 1555. Ridley suffered particularly horribly. (Kronheim print in *Pictures of English History from the Earliest Times*, c. 1892, plate XLVII.)

Fire being now put to him, he stretched out his right hand, and thrust it into the flame, and held it there a good space, before the fire came to any other part of his body; where his hand was seen of every man sensibly burning, crying with a loud voice, 'This hand hath offended'. As soon as the fire got up, he was very soon dead, never stirring or crying all the while'.

As much as one might admire the courage of these men, it should be pointed out that many were themselves deeply intolerant. Cranmer, for example, was fully implicated in the horrors perpetrated upon Catholics by Henry VIII.

The very last person to be burnt for heresy in England was an Anabaptist, who denied the Trinity and that Jesus was the son of God. Edward Wightman was burnt at Lichfield on 11 April 1612. Remarkably, this was his second burning. The first time, a few weeks previously, he had recanted at the stake as the flames licked around him and he had been dragged clear, 'well-scorched'. When he had recovered his courage however, he had repeated his heresies. Tied to the stake once more, he again attempted to recant but the irritated sheriff merely piled on more wood. Burning for heresy was finally abolished in 1677.

In the light of the zealotry with which heretics were pursued, it is surprising that there was not a more avid persecution of witches. In England, doubts about the actual existence of witchcraft meant that it was not until 1542 that the practice became a felony, though the relevant statute was repealed in 1547. The offence was restored in 1563, and Agnes Waterhouse, hanged at Chelmsford on 29 July 1566, was one of the first to suffer. Under common law, torture was not permitted in order to extract confessions

(though forms of coercion were employed) and accusations of witchcraft were really rather rare. For example, there were only 456 witchcraft cases heard in the assize courts of the counties of Essex, Hertfordshire, Surrey and Sussex between 1559 and 1736 – fewer than three a year. Furthermore, 55 per cent of defendants were acquitted, 21 per cent suffered a non-capital punishment and only 24 per cent were executed. However, of the 109 executions, 102 were of women.

The *Malleus Maleficarum* explained that a woman was 'more credulous ... more impressionable'; furthermore she was 'a liar by nature'. Such literature only partly explains why women were more vulnerable to accusations of witchcraft. Modern scholarship suggests that women were just as likely to be the accusers as the accused in witchcraft cases. Older, poorer, women, it has been argued, were particularly likely to be accused because they were marginalised, no longer economically productive and, therefore, perceived as a nuisance to the community.

Three of the witches of Northamptonshire, depicted riding a pig. From the title page of a contemporary account (coloured by hand).

It was in Scotland that witches were most enthusiastically persecuted, particularly after the Witchcraft Act of 1563. Religious reformers led the way, assisted by the fact that torture was permitted under Scottish law. In one Orkney case, thumbscrews were applied to a girl of just seven. Since confessions could be extracted by such means, conviction rates were much higher than in England. A survey of almost six hundred Scottish cases has shown that 55 per cent of those accused were executed and only 21 per cent completely acquitted. Surviving sources have led serious scholars to suggest that at least 1,500 people

The title page of a 1669 edition from Lyon of the *Malleus Maleficarum*, the 'Hammer of witches'. Written by Dominicans Jakob Sprenger and Heinrich Kramer and first published in 1486, this more than any other book was cited in order to justify the torture and execution of witches.

A witch feeds her familiars in 1579. From an engraving in *A Rehearsall at Winsore*, coloured by hand.

A miniature of James I (1566–1625), James VI of Scotland. (Attributed to Isaak Oliver or Nicholas Hilliard.)

The witches of North Berwick set fire to churches and cast spells to make cattle sick. (From James VI, *Newes from Scotland*, 1591.)

were executed as witches, considerably more than in the much more populous England. Scottish witches were burned but generally 'worried' or strangled first. Some, however, were 'burnt quick', that is, alive. In 1608 the Earl of Mar complained that some witches at Brechin, 'half-burnt', had 'broke out of the fire and were cast in quick while they were burnt to death'. The complex feuding within Scottish politics probably accounts for the fact that accusations of witchcraft were quite often levied at those high up in the social hierarchy. Most notoriously, Francis Stewart, the 5th Earl of Bothwell, was accused of employing witchcraft and plotting treason against James VI.

On 20 August 1589, James was married by proxy to Anne, Princess of Denmark, in Copenhagen. Anne then attempted to sail to Scotland to join James but storms forced her to land in Norway. James sailed to collect her, but on the way home another storm arose and their ship was nearly sunk. In the summer of 1590 a witch-hunt began in Denmark, during the course of which some of the accused confessed to having conjured up these storms. Hearing of the confessions, James suspected that enemies at home might also have conspired in the affair. He readily believed the confession of John Fian, a schoolteacher, who eventually admitted to a number of offences, including the raising of storms at a meeting of a coven of witches on Auld Kirk Green in North Berwick. Fian, whose legs were broken and finger nails ripped out, named others

After prolonged torture the North Berwick Witches, Agnes Sampson, Agnes Tompson, Dr Fian and others, were tried before King James. Most of them were executed. (From *Newes from Scotland*.)

and James personally supervised their subsequent interrogation at Holyrood House. Over sixty people, including Bothwell, were accused of participating in a vast diabolical conspiracy. Many went to the flames between 1591 and 1592 but Bothwell was not tried until 10 August 1593. He had influential supporters and was acquitted. In 1597, James penned a book, *Daemonologie*, affirming the existence of witches, describing their characteristics and supporting their suppression.

With such an endorsement Scottish persecution continued with vigour. Between 1661 and 1662 a witch scare began in East Lothian and Midlothian, sparked by the activities of professional 'prickers', witch-finders who pricked suspects and denounced them if their wound did not bleed. The persecution spread across Scotland and around 660 were accused. There were at least sixty-five executions, possibly many more.

English witch-hunts were tame by comparison. The largest single series of trials was that of the Pendle witches in August 1612. At least nineteen were accused and eight women and

The cover of *Daemonologie* by James I (1597).

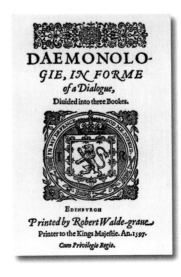

DAEMONOLO-
GIE, IN FORME
of a Dialogue,
Diuided into three Bookes.

EDINBVRGH
Printed by Robert Walde-graue,
Printer to the Kings Majestie. An.1597.
Cum Priuilegio Regio.

Joan Upney, Joan Prentice and Joan Cony are hanged at Chelmsford on 5 July 1589. Upney was accused of letting loose a plague of toads which bit and killed two people. Joan Prentice had given her soul to Satan, who had appeared to her in the shape of a ferret. From an anonymous pamphlet of 1598.

two men were eventually hanged. Witch trials occurred sporadically thereafter and the very last victims were probably the three women, the Bideford Witches, hanged at Heavitree, Exeter, on 25 August 1682. Alice Molland was sentenced to death at Exeter in 1684, but there is no evidence that the sentence was carried out. Jane Wenham was convicted in 1712, but reprieved. By now belief in witchcraft had waned among the English educated classes. Scotland however, retained its enthusiasm a little while longer. Janet Horne was the last person burnt as a Scottish witch. She was accused of having used her daughter as a flying pony in order to ride to the Devil. Stripped, smothered in tar and paraded through Dornoch on a barrel, she was burned alive in June 1727. In 1736, however, an Act of Parliament declared that 'No prosecution ... suit or proceedings, shall be commenced against any person for Witchcraft, Sorcery, Inchantment or Conjuration.' This however, was not quite the end. The very last person to be 'executed' for witchcraft might be said to be Ruth Osborne, who was drowned illegally by a mob at Tring in Hertfordshire in 1751 – on this occasion, the leader of the mob, Thomas Colley, was hanged.

Hanging was much the most common form of execution in Britain. For a time however it was rivalled in the North by decapitation, performed by a form of guillotine. A device was set up in Halifax, Yorkshire, in the early Tudor period and continued to function until 1650. It is said to have inspired a similar device, 'The Maiden', set up in Edinburgh and now preserved in the National Museum of Scotland. Scotland's machine was first used in 1564 and dispatched at least 150 people before it was withdrawn in 1708.

Hanging was neither as visually spectacular as decapitation, nor as gruesome, but it was probably less humane. V. A. C. Gatrell has identified some 1,035 executions in England and Wales between 1805 and 1818 alone. Of these, 216 were for burglary or housebreaking, 204 for forgery, 202 for murder, 116 for simple robbery and 82 for horse, sheep or cattle theft. English criminal law at this time was still disfigured by the so-called 'Bloody Code'. The Restoration in 1688 had been a triumph of the landed aristocracy over the king and one consequence was a long series of capital statutes designed to protect their property. Under the Black Act (9 Geo. 1 c. 22) of 1723 it became a capital offence to go disguised, 'blacked', or armed, in royal forests, to kill cattle, set fire to corn, haystacks, barns or other buildings.

The Act introduced more than fifty criminal offences: other statutes followed. By the end of the eighteenth century, the Bloody Code included well over two hundred offences. One could be executed for stealing goods valued at more than twelve pence, for theft from dyeing or bleaching grounds, for arson, for passing forged notes, for damaging trees and many other crimes besides. The consequence was a criminal justice system which, by European standards, seemed peculiarly addicted to putting people to death. As Gatrell observes, the number of executions in the whole of Prussia in the 1770s rarely exceeded fifteen a year. If we take London alone however, the gruesome total between 1774 and 1777 amounted to 139 executions, whereas in Paris over the same period there were only thirty-two.

There were, of course, other ways in which premature extinction could occur within the criminal justice system. Conditions in prison were harsh. At the Black Assizes of 1750, death sentences were passed upon two prisoners who were already dying of 'gaol fever' (typhus). This promptly spread through the courtroom, killing the judge, jury and legal officers.

The Halifax
'Guillotine' from
Hone's *Table Book*,
Vol. I, 1837.

Preparations for the hanging of Stephen Gardiner at Tyburn in 1724. He is already dressed in his death shroud, as the sheriff looks on and prepares to give the signal. (Unattributed engraving.)

Opposite: Two offenders pilloried at Charing Cross in 1809. A large crowd has gathered to enjoy the spectacle. (Aquatint by Thomas Rowlandson and A. C. Pugin for Ackermann's *Microcosm of London*, 1808–10.)

Those who were not jailed were sometimes pilloried and, depending upon the offence, this could amount to little more than a quasi-judicial execution. The pillory was used to punish offences such as petty theft or the use of dishonest weights and measures, for perjurers, for writers or publishers of seditious libels, and for those convicted of sexual offences. The punishment inflicted depended almost entirely on the caprice of the mob. The libeller, Thomas Dangerfield, was killed by a blow to the head on his way back from the pillory in 1685, whereas, when Daniel Defoe was exhibited for the same offence in 1703, he was garlanded with flowers and plied with drink. Where the crime had particularly outraged popular morality, the offender was at risk of being battered to death by stones or else literally smothered by the filth. Count von Archenholz wrote in his memoirs that the punishment for 'unnatural vice' was the pillory but, 'With this accusation, it is, however, better to suffer death at once; for, on such an occasion, the fury of the populace is unbounded, and even the better sort of people have no compassion for the culprit.' There were many fatalities – John Middleton, for example, was killed in the pillory in 1723 – but even survivors suffered horrendous injuries. Anne Marrow, a bigamist, lost both eyes in the pillory in 1777. The arbitrary nature of the punishment finally led to its abolition in 1837.

*Fig. 57.—Captain Dangerfield in the Pillory.*

Captain Dangerfield in the Pillory; shortly after leaving it, he was killed by a blow to the head. (Woodcut by an unnamed artist in the *Roxburghe Ballads*, Vol. 5, part 1, page 174.)

# THE CREATURES OF THE
SCAFFOLD

IT IS SOMEWHAT to the defence of the criminal justice system of the time that it was not entirely partial in its application. Sometimes even wealthy and well-connected men were hanged. Most notable was Laurence Shirley, the 4th Earl Ferrers, executed in 1760 for the murder of a family steward. Most of the condemned, however, came from the lower and most desperate classes. Until 1836, defendants in felony (that is, capital) cases were not allowed defence counsel. While incarcerated they had great difficulty in summoning defence witnesses and trials were brief. In July 1832, a schoolmaster wrote to *Frasers' Magazine* about his experiences at Newgate Prison.

> Seeing their fellow prisoners return tried and found guilty in a minute or two after having been taken up, they become so alarmed and nervous ... they lose all command over themselves, and are then, to use their own language, taken up to be knocked down like bullocks unheard ... two-thirds of the prisoners, cannot tell of any thing which has passed in the court, not even, very frequently, whether they have been tried.

Some of these unfortunates were very young. John Dean was allegedly aged only eight or nine when he was hanged for arson in 1629. The absence of reliable records at that time makes it difficult to authenticate this and other claims, but Home Office records do show that Baron Hotham condemned a ten-year-old boy to death for stealing at Chelmsford Post Office in 1800. In court the boy looked 'an absolute child' and Hotham was forced by the jury and crowd to consider mercy. In the end the defendant was transported for fourteen years. A fourteen-year-old, John Bell, was actually hanged for murder at Maidstone Prison in 1831. The crime was indeed atrocious but the executioner himself was horrified and described the body swaying, 'to and fro, dead as the feelings of an English judge.' There are many authenticated accounts of teenagers of fifteen or sixteen being hanged.

John Bell at least died quickly on the 'new drop' at Maidstone. As previously mentioned, slow strangulation was the fate of many and, in

Opposite:
*Under The Scaffold,*
*or The Hangman's*
*Pupils,* a satire
on the fascination
with public
executions.
(Matt Morgan in
*The Tomahawk,*
26 October 1867.)

The Old Bailey (London's Central Criminal Court) in 1809. Trials, even capital trials, usually took just a few minutes, and juries often gave their verdicts without retiring. (Illustration by Pugin and Rowlandson.)

London, this most famously occurred at Tyburn's Triple Tree, located either near today's Marble Arch or a little to the north-west at Connaught Square. Each of its three cross-beams was about 9 feet long and stood on legs 18 feet high. It was erected in 1571 and could accommodate up to twenty-four felons at a time – though only in 1649 was this tested. The tree was taken down in 1759 for the rather mundane planning reason that it was obstructing traffic. A mobile gallows was employed in its place. Until 1783, when the place of execution was moved to outside Newgate Prison, executions at Tyburn were preceded by a riotous procession which left Newgate, went first to the Church of St Sepulchre, then through Holborn and down what is today Oxford Street. The journey could take up to two hours, with the condemned accompanied by their own coffins. By tradition they were passed drinks on their journey and the procession moved along with much buffoonery, the crowd being taken full advantage of both by prostitutes and pick-pockets.

For the condemned, the period leading up to their deaths was often the only time in their wretched lives when they were the centre of attention. Some, such as Dick Turpin, who was executed at York racecourse on 7 April 1739, became celebrities and their exploits were rapidly romanticised.

Jack Sheppard, whose portrait was commissioned in 1724, became one of many felons thus depicted. Such men held court and lived well, for a time. Most felons, however, merely went to a shabby end, and an attempt to die well and with dignity was all that was left to them. Elizabeth Fry found that a condemned woman in Newgate generally occupied her time by thinking about her 'appearance on the scaffold, the dress in which she shall be hanged'. William Hepworth Dixon reported that, when a man remained defiant to the end in 1848, his mother cried out 'Bravo, I knew he would die game!' A party of his friends went to the pub afterwards in his memory.

In the eighteenth century the ever-increasing number of offences for which one might be hanged and the decline of torturous punishments had posed something of a problem for the authorities. How was the punishment of a murderer to be distinguished from that of a mere thief? The answer had been found in the 1752 Murder Act, which had regularised the practice of either having the body of a murderer anatomised (dissected) by the surgeons, or else hung in irons on a public gibbet. Dishonouring the body after death was a fearsome prospect in a Christian society in which many believed that, without a proper burial, the deceased would be denied resurrection. The authorities then were able to stigmatise the murderer and they were also able to solve a practical educational difficulty.

By the eighteenth century the expanding medical schools were finding it difficult to procure enough corpses required in order to teach anatomy. Only half a dozen or so bodies of felons were permitted by Elizabethan statutes to

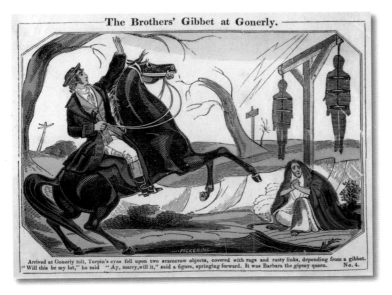

The Brothers' Gibbet at Gonerly.

Arrived at Gonerly hill, Turpin's eyes fell upon two scarecrow objects, covered with rags and rusty links, depending from a gibbet. "Will this be my lot," he said   "Ay, marry, will it," said a figure, springing forward. It was Barbara the gipsey queen.    No. 4.

Left: A depiction of Dick Turpin riding past The Brothers' Gibbet at Gonerly, where a gypsy foretells his own fate. (Unknown artist, the Bruce Castle Museum.)

Following pages: The Tyburn Procession in 1747 as depicted in *The Idle 'Prentice Hanged at Tyburn* by William Hogarth.

37

Design'd & Engrav'd by W<sup>m</sup> Hogarth

The last dying
Speech & Confession
of T. Idle

Verf: 27,28.)
n, and their
wind: when
hen they shall
ot answer.

Publish'd according to Act of Parliam.t Sep.30. 174

An engraving of
the dissection
of a felon by
William Hogarth
in his series
*The Rewards of
Cruelty*, 1750–1.

be sent to the College of Surgeons. Sending the bodies of most murderers would, it was hoped, alleviate this problem. The prospect struck terror into the condemned and something of that feeling can be seen Hogarth's graphic depiction of do ctors gathered like vultures and leering over a corpse. However, there were still not enough corpses and the medical schools were forced into shady relationships with 'resurrectionists' in order to secure them. These men would dig up fresh corpses from graveyards and sell them on. Stealing corpses became known as 'burking' after William Burke and William Hare were discovered to have gone one step further, by murdering the living in order to sell their remains. The fate of Hare is unknown but Burke was executed and dissected in Edinburgh in 1829. Body snatching abated after 1832, when a thoughtful piece of legislation saved the graves of the well-off by allowing the unclaimed bodies of the deceased from workhouses to be sent for anatomisation instead.

Gibbetting was intended to make a permanent and public display of the consequences of crime. The body would be tarred after death and then hung in chains to preserve it on the gibbet for as long as possible. Such exhibitions attracted substantial crowds. It is said that 100,000 came to see the body of Lewis Avershaw gibbetted on Wimbledon Common in 1795. Somewhat surprisingly, in folk belief, objects associated with execution were often supposed to be lucky or have curative powers. Thus Northumbrians would cure toothache with a splinter of wood from Winters Gibbet on Elsdon Moor, and in Durham a shaving from the gibbet on Ferry Hill was similarly employed. The display of the felon however, ended in 1832.

The size of the crowd on the day of execution itself exceeded the number gathered at any one time around the gibbet. The crowd at the execution of Dr Dodd in 1777 was said to have been one of the largest gatherings London had ever seen. Dodd was a gentleman, a clergyman and a philanthropist, but, after a sensational trial, he was convicted of forging a bond and thus became a celebrity candidate for the rope. A petition with thousands of signatures failed to gain him a reprieve and he was dispatched at Tyburn on 27 June 1777. Few executions attracted such interest but Barry Faulk has written that, 'To write a history of capital punishment in England is to write a history of festive life'. For many, an execution signalled a holiday: schoolboys in Reading were given the day off to see the salutary display and London

Below, left:
A body gibbet and pillory, preserved at the Old Court Hall, Winchelsea, Sussex. The iron cage is capped with the skull of John Breeds, a butcher hanged in 1742.

Below:
'The Gallows' as depicted by Jouve in L'Assiette au Beurre, 23 November 1901.

apprentices enjoyed a similar privilege. The crowd was often raucous and was well-catered-for by food vendors, publicans, quack doctors, entertainers, hawkers of broadsheets, and procurers, among others.

Everyone did not, of course, mix together indiscriminately. The wealthier classes rented windows overlooking the scaffold. At Tyburn they could reserve places on temporary seating erected for the spectacle. By the second half of the nineteenth century, however, it was not quite respectable for gentlemen to attend executions. In 1868 *The Tomahawk* described these gentlemen spectators as 'The swells – the dissipated government clerks and fast young attorneys, the whisker-less subalterns seeing the first of life and the wig-wearing fogies watching the last of it'. Few spectators would admit to being motivated by the feelings that inspired the eighteenth-century MP George Augustus Selwyn to tour executions. Selwyn travelled to the continent to witness torture on the scaffold and allegedly dressed up in women's clothes to avoid being recognised among the crowds, a ruse that only made sense if, as many sources attest, many women indeed attended.

The behaviour of the crowd at the moment of execution itself was much disputed throughout the nineteenth century. Charles Dickens, who was opposed to public execution, claimed that at the execution of the poisoner François Courvoisier, he had observed 'No sorrow, no salutary terror, no abhorrence, no seriousness; nothing but ribaldry, debauchery, levity, drunkenness and flaunting vice in fifty other shapes.' On the other hand, the Reverend J. Davis, who supported the practice, informed a capital punishment commission in 1866 that he had officiated at twenty-four executions and at the final moments 'the behaviour of the crowd is as solemn as it can be.' There is much evidence on both sides and modern readers will perhaps not be surprised that different newspapers reported the same execution quite differently, depending upon their stance on the subject as a whole. One thing, however, is clear; the crowd could turn hostile very quickly if the procedure itself was botched by the executioner.

Thus far we have observed some of the punishments visited on wrong-doers, but who were the men employed to carry them out? For most of British history, to be an executioner was not merely to hang felons, but also to whip, burn and mutilate bodies. Such a man was generally shunned, in particular by the very people who employed him. Certainly, the British executioner was a man of low social status and was, for the most part, badly paid. Generally, executioners were not salaried employees; rather, they were men who worked on a fee-per-job basis. Even into the 1920s the fee was a mere £10 in England and a more generous £15 in Scotland.

Executioners in the eighteenth century and before supplemented their fees by selling souvenirs such as pieces of the rope and other artefacts associated with notorious felons. The belief that the touch of a hanged man would cure skin diseases allowed executioners to charge sufferers for mounting the scaffold and many a young child was carried up to touch a swinging corpse. During the nineteenth century, the 'perks' of the executioner were steadily removed. Those active in London tended to be the busiest, but as the number of executions declined, many counties ceased to have their own executioners. An executioner would thus be sent out from London to perform the occasional provincial appointment. Notwithstanding their popular notoriety, such executioners were only temporarily employed at the whim of the Home Office and selected upon each occasion from a list. Although some attempted to give themselves some species of official status, there was in effect no single official state executioner appointed as the nation's lethal civil servant.

THE HANGMAN.

A hangman of 1840, depicted by Kenny Meadows in *Heads of the People*.

The money earned by executioners had always been inadequate and those who wanted respectability and stability had to pursue a regular occupation between executions. But many were not respectable. Some came to the trade to avoid the noose themselves. During the reign of Charles II, a man and his two sons were convicted of horse-stealing at Derby. All were condemned but a pardon was offered to any one of them who would hang the other two. The father and older brother declined, but the younger brother took the offer with alacrity and thereafter served as the county's favoured executioner. Similarly, in 1731, a Matthew Blackbourn was convicted of a capital offence at York, but received a pardon on condition of serving as hangman. There were many hangmen who were convicted felons and who continued in their old ways while 'on the books'. For example, in *The Hangmen of England* Victor Bailey notes that Pascha Rose, himself a hangman, was hanged at Tyburn in 1686 for housebreaking; another, John Price, was hanged at Bunwell in 1718 for attempted rape. One of his successors, William Marvel, was transported in 1719 for stealing silk handkerchiefs. John Thrift, another eighteenth-century hangman, was found guilty of murder; Edward Dennis of larceny: the list goes on. Men either came to the job desperate or became desperate in the job. Many were heavy drinkers and lived a low life, but not necessarily through choice. Coaches would not carry executioners for fear of the ill luck that they carried; respectable people would not associate with them; and if the more enterprising of them carried on small independent businesses as cobblers, carpenters, publicans and the like, it was for a good reason – few people wanted to employ them.

The most famous executioner of all was Jack Ketch (active 1663–86), whose name became a synonym for subsequent hangmen. No portrait survives, but a contemporary woodcut from 1678 (see contents page) shows a man being drawn to Tyburn to be hanged, drawn and quartered declaring 'I am sick of a traytorous disease.' Jack Ketch stands alongside him, brandishing an axe and a rope and declaring 'Here's your cure, sir!' One notices that Ketch is not wearing a mask. While a number of authentic metal executioners' masks survive from Europe and some are exhibited in the Science Museum, the only known British example is probably a misidentification of a scold's bridle used to silence nagging women. British masks were probably cloth or leather and have not survived. It is sometimes supposed that the executioner's mask, which has become in the popular imagination an iconic symbol of his profession, was intended to prevent the executioner being identified and suffering reprisals. This is rather suspect – certainly in respect of Britain. Some wore masks, some did not: furthermore, some seem to have slipped them on only when beginning their work – by which time, of course, the crowd had already had a good look at them. Many British executioners seem rather to have revelled in their notoriety, or else used their 'fame' as a tool in touting for business or disposing of gallows souvenirs. Perhaps a better explanation is that the mask was a relic of an earlier theatrical and more torturous age; one of the accoutrements of horror to accompany the torture and final despatch of the victim. It served to disguise the emotion of the executioner going about his work – whether it be pity which might undermine the legitimacy of the punishment or sadistic glee, which might detract from its moral purpose. Certainly, after 1868, masks were abandoned in Britain. Accoutrements of horror merely made an execution more difficult and, whatever their actual competence, late Victorian executioners liked to portray themselves as considerate, businesslike men, arranging affairs with as little fuss as possible. William Marwood remarked upon the benefits of such an approach that 'Whenever I tap a prisoner on the shoulder he nearly always comes to me.'

Back in the seventeenth century, however, men such as Ketch were still engaged to inflict pain upon their victims as well as dispatch them. Even where that was not the intent, their competence was doubtful. Whatever his skills as a hangman, Ketch was notoriously maladroit with an axe. On 21 July 1683 he was employed to behead Lord Russell, who had been convicted of a plot to assassinate Charles II. Russell paid him well for a swift kill, but Ketch's first blow was wholly inadequate and Russell is said to have declared 'You dog, did I give you ten guineas to use me so inhumanely!' It took three more blows to sever Russell's head. When, in 1685, Ketch dispatched the Duke of Monmouth, Monmouth took the precaution of giving some money to a servant to pass on to the executioner if the job was done well. On the scaffold he fingered the axe and remarked 'I fear that it is not sharp enough.' Perhaps the Duke was right, for the first blow merely wounded him. The Duke half-rose and placed his neck again on the block. After two more blows the head was still not off and the body was quivering. Two more blows brought release to the Duke, though his head had still to be cut through with a knife. We do not know whether or not Ketch received his tip.

Executions were still being botched in the nineteenth century. No drop was allowed at Robert Johnston's hanging in Edinburgh in 1818. He was left strangling on tip-toe while the executioner and sheriff were pelted. Johnston was cut down and taken away by the crowd. The authorities recovered him and he was taken back to the scaffold by soldiers and then dispatched. When John Tapner was hanged in Guernsey in 1854, the executioner failed to pinion his arms securely. The drop was short and as Tapner dangled on the end of the rope he managed to free an arm. He tried to pull himself up and spectators reported that he managed to get an elbow through the trap before the Deputy Sheriff knocked it away. The executioner was ordered to pull on Tapner's legs and the Sheriff was able to report to the Home Office that 'The sufferings of the culprit did not last for more than four minutes after the trap fell … I am satisfied that the struggles of the culprit were not greater, nor more prolonged, than is usual upon such occasions'.

Such occasions were becoming less frequent and in 1832, a Whig administration abolished the death penalty for stealing from houses, coining, and stealing livestock. Increasingly, juries could not be persuaded to convict defendants of capital offences, especially where only loss to property was involved. Further reforms to the capital statutes followed and, although capital punishment remained on the statute books for offences such as treason or piracy, in practice the number of public executions had slowed to a mere trickle of unreprieved murderers. Furthermore, the Capital Punishment Amendment Act 1868 abolished public execution. There were those who argued that the sight of the gallows was the only sure deterrent but Victorian sensibility would no longer tolerate felons being strangled in public, nor crowds of uncertain temper in middle-class districts disturbing commerce and scandalising the respectable. The very last person to be executed publicly in England was Michael Barratt, an Irish nationalist who planted a bomb outside Clerkenwell Prison in order to free Irish prisoners. Twelve people died as a result and Barratt was turned off on a mobile scaffold erected outside Newgate Prison on 26 May 1868. Henceforth, executions took place within prison walls, witnessed only by officials and (in the early years) gentlemen of the press. The question for abolitionists was whether this change was a step on the way to the total abolition of capital punishment or whether the ability to conduct executions in private might only serve to encourage it.

*The Cure for Murder, or Justice clings to the Gallows.* Justice clings to the gallows as the only proper punishment for those who have committed murder. A satire against those who wanted to abolish capital punishment. (Matt Morgan in *The Tomahawk,* 23 October 1869.)

THE CURE FOR MURDER!
JUSTICE CLINGS TO THE GALLOWS.

## Pendaison d'une femme, en Angleterre

Louise Masset éxécutée dans la prison de Newgate.

# THE SLOW DEATH
# OF HANGING

I now hold that the law of capital punishment falls with terrible weight upon the hangman and to allow a man to follow such an occupation is doing him a deadly wrong.

So WROTE Henry Berry in 1905. Berry is remembered as one of the most humane and conscientious of British hangmen, though even his record was far from spotless. In November 1885, in the first year of his career, he allowed too long a drop when hanging Robert Goodale at Norwich for the murder of his wife. The result was that Goodale's head became detached. As there were no longer any public witnesses and with the horrors of the execution out of sight, many of the abolitionist organisations that had been influential prior to 1868 went into decline. Yet, within the penal establishment, people began to consider the effect that carrying out sentences had on those called upon to implement them. Albert Pierrepoint, who served as a hangman from 1932 to 1956, later wrote of having 'seen prison officers faint upon the scaffold, strong men weep, and women prison officers sobbing helplessly.' When a woman was to be hanged, the female prison officers did not enter the execution chamber, being replaced by male officers, but the effect of an execution upon a whole prison establishment was described as 'dismal'. Pierrepoint himself made a point that others endorsed: 'All the men and women whom I have faced at that final moment convince me that in what I have done I have not prevented a single murder'. Whereas an offence such as armed robbery might be considered one of calculation, many murders are, in fact, committed in a heat of passion wherein the culprit does not consider future consequences at all. It need hardly be pointed out that European states that have abolished the death penalty have very much lower homicide rates than many jurisdictions that retain it.

Moves to limit the use of capital punishment had begun much earlier in other European jurisdictions than in Britain. For example, as early as 1794 Prussia had restricted the death penalty to murder alone. In the twentieth century, the Scandinavian countries led the way towards complete abolition.

Opposite:
A depiction of the hanging at Newgate in 1900 of Louise Masset for killing her five-year-old son. Note there are no female officers present. (P. H. Ripp in L'espress de Lyon Illustré, 28 January 1900.)

Dr Hawley Harvey
Crippen. (*The
Sketch*, 1910.)

The death penalty was abolished for all offences in peacetime in Norway in 1902 and there were no executions in Sweden after 1910. British colonies sometimes proved more amenable to abolition than the mother country and Queensland was one of the first, abolishing hanging in 1922. At home, however, British public opinion remained in favour of capital punishment, as did a significant constituency within the police and judiciary. Notorious killers retained, as they do today, a species of celebrity and there was much public satisfaction at their judicial disposal.

Hawley Harvey Crippen was one such. A Michigan-born homeopath and distributor of patent medicines, Crippen married a music-hall singer, Corrine 'Cora' Turner, in the United States in 1894. The marriage was unhappy, Cora was unfaithful and when they came to England Crippen met a typist, Ethel Le Neve. The girl became his mistress in 1908 and Crippen plotted Cora's demise. Cora disappeared in January 1910 and Crippen claimed that she had returned home. Unfortunately for him, another music-hall entertainer who knew Cora became suspicious and she happened to be married to a superintendent at Scotland Yard. Crippen's house was searched but nothing was found. The matter would probably have rested there had Crippen not panicked. He and Le Neve, disguised as a boy, fled to Antwerp and boarded a liner, the *Montrose*, bound for Quebec. The authorities then conducted a more thorough search and found the remains of Cora's body in the cellar. On board the *Montrose* the captain had, meanwhile, become suspicious and while just within range of the new radio transmitters, was able to send a message to London. Chief Inspector Walter Drew was able to board a faster liner, the *Laurentic*, and so arrive in Canada ahead of Crippen. Returned home, Crippen was found guilty in just twenty-seven minutes and executed on 23 November 1910 at Pentonville Prison. Le Neve was charged with being an accessory after the fact, but remarkably was acquitted.

It seems fair to assert that there was some sympathy for women in the criminal justice system; after all, the ideology of the time suggested that they were the weaker sex and prone to be led astray. Certainly, there was a reluctance to execute women and between 1907 and 1922 no woman was executed in England. Then came the disturbing case of Edith Thompson. Born of respectable family, by 1922 Edith was a buyer for a millinery firm and settled in one of the better streets of Ilford with her husband Percy. Percy did not treat her well and in 1920 she met Freddy Bywaters, an eighteen-year-old seaman. They had an affair, which Percy discovered. On 3 October 1922,

Opposite:
Dr Crippen
is hanged at
Pentonville, 23
November 1910.
(*Le petit Parisien*,
11 December
1910.)

Percy was set upon and fatally stabbed after returning from the theatre. Edith had been present and subsequently named Freddy as the assailant. However, a search of Freddy's possessions revealed a collection of love letters from Edith.

Edith Thompson is executed at Holloway Prison for the murder of her husband. The true circumstances of the execution were rather more horrific than the image suggests. (Illustration by Andre Gallard in *Le Petit Journal*, 21 January 1923.)

**Le Petit Journal**

HEBDOMADAIRE
61, rue Lafayette, Paris ===== *illustré* ===== PRIX : **0 fr. 30**
21 Janvier 1923

12 Pages — 12 Pages

**Une Femme expie son crime**

En Grande-Bretagne la justice a gardé son caractère tragiquement désuet et les criminels y sont pendus. Mme Thompson, qui assassina son mari, a été exécutée dans sa prison, malgré de nombreuses pétitions qui demandaient une commutation de peine.

It was alleged that Edith had had a common purpose to procure the death of Percy and she was charged with murder. The case was circumstantial and in court the judge dwelt heavily on the immorality of adultery, as though that was the subject of the trial, and not the murder. Edith herself appeared in her own defence and appeared glib and overconfident of acquittal. Many, including Edith, were surprised when she was convicted. The public mood, which had been hostile to her at first, now swung behind her and a petition for clemency quickly gathered thousands of signatures. It was not heeded and, at 9 a.m. on 9 January 1923, Edith was hanged in Holloway Prison. Freddy was executed at the same time in nearby Pentonville.

Freddy maintained to the end that Edith was innocent and the manner of her execution became something of a scandal. An hysterical Edith had to be dragged to the gallows by four wardens. Accounts of what followed are contradictory, but one version asserts that she then collapsed and had to be hanged while tied on a chair. It was alleged that she suffered massive internal bleeding, leading some to suggest that she might have been pregnant at the time. Whatever the truth, the effect upon the presiding officials is well documented. The prison chaplain suffered a nervous breakdown and resigned. A witness giving evidence to the Royal Commission on Capital Punishment in 1950 said of the governor that she 'had never seen a person so changed in appearance by mental suffering as the governor appeared to me to be'. Two of the wardens attending went to see Beverley Baxter, MP, to plead for abolition and Baxter said to the House of Commons later, 'Their faces were not human. I can assure you, they were like people out of another world.' And still the executions went on.

Nevertheless, there was gathering opposition in Parliament to the death penalty. In 1930 a House of Commons Select Committee recommended a five-year suspension of executions. In 1938, the House of Commons carried a motion calling for the same. With the war the issue was sidelined, but in 1948 the Commons narrowly passed a bill, again asking for a five-year suspension. The Lords threw it out; the bishops being prominent in the argument in favour of capital punishment. On the continent meanwhile, the horrors of war and the abuses perpetrated by totalitarian regimes had turned opinion in the newly reconstituted states decisively against execution. After a round of executions for war crimes, there were no further executions in Italy after 1947 (although it remained a possibility in law) and capital punishment was forbidden in 1949 under the constitution of the new West Germany. Switzerland had already abolished it after a referendum in 1944. Although capital punishment remained on the statute books of other countries, there was an increasing tendency to commute death sentences to life imprisonment. Yet in Britain, in the context of a general increase in crime, a section of public opinion remained convinced of the deterrent effect of the hangman and it was only after a number of controversial executions that the demand for change became inexorable.

In November 1949, Timothy John Evans was arrested for the murder of his wife, Beryl, and their baby, Geraldine, after their bodies were found at his address in Ladbroke Grove in London. Evans, who had learning difficulties, confessed under police interrogation to the murder of the child. He subsequently retracted that confession, but nonetheless was hanged at Pentonville Prison on 9 March 1950. A key witness in the case against him was John Reginald Christie, who lived at the same address. But in 1953, Christie was convicted of the murder of his own wife and confessed to the murder of five more women whose remains were found at the house. These women had been killed over a ten-year period and all had been strangled,

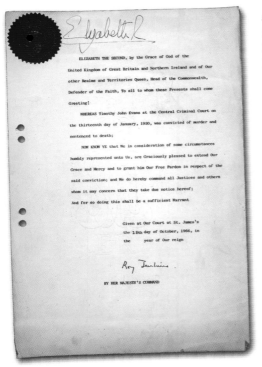

*E wabeth R*

ELIZABETH THE SECOND, by the Grace of God of the United Kingdom of Great Britain and Northern Ireland and of Our other Realms and Territories Queen, Head of the Commonwealth, Defender of the Faith, To all to whom these Presents shall come Greeting!

WHEREAS Timothy John Evans at the Central Criminal Court on the thirteenth day of January, 1950, was convicted of murder and sentenced to death;

NOW KNOW YE that We in consideration of some circumstances humbly represented unto Us, are Graciously pleased to extend Our Grace and Mercy and to grant him Our Free Pardon in respect of the said conviction; and We do hereby command all Justices and others whom it may concern that they take due notice hereof;

And for so doing this shall be a sufficient Warrant

Given at Our Court at St. James's the 18th day of October, 1966, in the     year of Our reign

*Roy Jenkins*

BY HER MAJESTY'S COMMAND

The posthumous royal pardon for Timothy John Evans, after his conviction for murder, signed by Roy Jenkins and Queen Elizabeth II 1966.

as had Beryl and Geraldine Evans. The irresistible inference was that Christie had killed those two as well as the other six and that Evans's confession had been obtained under duress. Christie was hanged at Pentonville on 15 July 1953. However, it took two inquiries before it was accepted that Evans had been wrongfully hanged and he was posthumously granted a free pardon in 1966.

Two further cases subsequently galvanised the abolitionist movement. The first was that of Derek Bentley. Bentley had been engaged in a burglary on the roof of a London warehouse when he had been grabbed by a policeman. Bentley had been accompanied by sixteen-year-old Christopher Craig. According to police, Bentley had shouted 'Let him have it, Chris!' whereupon Craig had fired a revolver and wounded the arresting officer. He had subsequently opened fire again and killed another policeman. It was claimed that Bentley had encouraged the shooting and both were convicted of murder. Craig was too young to be sentenced to death and Bentley himself was of limited mental capacity – he had made no attempt to use the knife with which he himself was armed, had denied shouting the words alleged and he had not, of course, fired the fatal shot. Two hundred MPs signed a petition calling for clemency but the Home Secretary refused to consider it and Bentley was hanged at Wandsworth Prison on 28 January 1953. Doubts about a confession made by Bentley, about ballistic evidence and about his fitness to stand trial contributed to the quashing of his murder conviction by the Court of Appeal in 1998.

In legal terms, the case of the nightclub hostess Ruth Ellis, who shot dead her violent former lover, David Blakely, outside a Hampstead pub in April 1955, was rather different. She undoubtedly intended the killing, but her own mental state and degree of culpability were called into question after it was discovered that she had suffered a miscarriage in January of that year following an assault by Blakely. In many eyes Blakely could scarcely be described as an innocent victim and, although by the standards of the time Ellis's sexual life was rather shocking, she was nevertheless young, pretty and a mother of two, all facts calculated to incite public sympathy. For her own part, Ellis made no attempt to deny guilt, declared her readiness to die and, perhaps crucially, protected her current lover, who had both driven her to the place where Blakely was shot and supplied the gun. Had she not done so, she might well have been reprieved. Nonetheless, more than fifty thousand people signed a petition calling for clemency and thirty-five members of the London County Council pleaded with the House of Commons to intervene. The use of a firearm, and the fact that a passer by was slightly injured by a stray bullet, induced the Home Office to reject these appeals and at Holloway Prison, at 9 a.m. on 13 July 1955, Ellis became the last woman to be hanged in Great Britain.

By 1956, the law was under urgent review. No one was hanged in Britain that year, but opposition in the Lords prevented a further attempt at abolition. As a compromise measure, the 1957 Homicide Act came into force. This retained the death penalty for five categories of murder, including murder of a policeman, murder of a prison officer, murder by shooting or causing explosions, murder while resisting or preventing lawful arrest and murder in the course of theft. The very last people to be executed in Britain under this Act were Peter Anthony Allen and Gwynne Owen Evans, hanged on 13 August 1964 at Liverpool and Manchester respectively, for the murder of a laundry van driver during a robbery. The Murder (Abolition of the Death Penalty) Act 1965 suspended the death sentence for murder for a period of five years and in 1969 this was made permanent. Technically, the death penalty was still available for high treason and piracy with violence, but these too were made non-capital in the Crime and Disorder Act 1998. Finally it was done.

Ruth Ellis was hanged on 11 July 1955, the last woman to be executed in Britain. (*The Illustrated London News*.)

# FURTHER READING

Bailey, B. *The Hangmen of England: A History of Execution from Jack Ketch to Albert Pierrepoint*. W. H. Allen, 1989.

Cooper, D. *The Lesson of the Scaffold: The Public Execution Controversy in Victorian England*. Allen Lane, 1974.

Emsley, C. *The English and Violence Since 1750*. Hambledon, 2005.

Gatrell, V. A. C. *The Hanging Tree: Execution and the English People, 1770–1868*. Oxford University Press, 1994.

Halliday, S. *Newgate: London's Prototype of Hell*. Sutton, 2006.

Potter, H. *Hanging in Judgment: Religion and the Death Penalty in England*. Continuum, 1993.

Sanson, H. *Executioners All: Memoirs of the Sansons from Private Notes and Documents, 1688–1847*. Spearman, 1962.

Spierenburg, P. *The Broken Spell: A Cultural and Anthropological History of Pre-Industrial Europe*. Rutgers University Press, 1991.

# PLACES TO VISIT

*The Blackpool Tower Dungeon*, Bank Hey Street, Blackpool, FY1 5BJ.
Telephone: 01253 622242.
Website: www.the-dungeons.co.uk/Blackpool

*Blicking Hall* (Birthplace of Anne Boleyn), Blickling, Norwich, NR11 6NF.
Telephone: 01263 738030.
Website: www.nationaltrust.org.uk/blickling

*Carisbrooke Castle Museum*, Newport, PO30 1XY.
Telephone: 01983 523112.
Website: www.carisbrookecastlemuseum.org.uk

*Clink Prison Museum*, 1 Clink Street, London SE1 9DG.
Telephone: 0207 4030900. Website: www.clink.co.uk

*Dartmoor Prison Museum*, HMP Dartmoor, Princetown, Devon, PL20 6RR.
Telephone: 01822 322130. Website: www.dartmoor-prison.co.uk

*The Edinburgh Dungeon*, 31 Market Street, Edinburgh, EH1 1DF.
Telephone: 01312 401001.
Website: www.the-dungeons.co.uk/edinburgh/en

*Galleries of Justice Museum*, The Lace Market, Nottingham, NG1 1HN.
Telephone: 01159 520555. Website: www.galleriesofjustice.org.uk

*Hampton Court Palace*, Surrey, KT8 9AU. Telephone: 08444 827777.
Website: www.hrp.org.uk/HamptonCourtPalace

*Hever Castle* (home of Anne Boleyn), Hever, nr Edenbridge, Kent, TN8 7NG. Telephone: 01732 865224. Website: www.hevercastle.co.uk

*Inveraray Jail*, Church Square, Inveraray, Argyll, PA32 8TX.
Telephone: 01499 302381. Website: http://www.inverarayjail.co.uk

*Jedburgh Castle Jail and Museum*, Castlegate, Jedburgh, Scottish Borders,
TD8 6QD. Telephone: 01835 863254.
Website: www.museumsgalleriesscotland.org.uk/member/jedburgh-castle-jail-and-museum

*Kensington Palace*, Kensington Gardens, London, W8 4PX.
Telephone: 08444 827777.
Website: www.hrp.org.uk/KensingtonPalace

*Lancaster Castle Prison*, Castle Parade, Lancaster LA1 1YJ.
Telephone: 01524 64998. Website: www.lancastercastle.com

*Lincoln Castle Prison and Museum*, Castle Hill, Lincoln, LN1 3AA.
Telephone: 01522 782040.
Website: www.lincolnshire.gov.uk/visiting/historic-buildings/lincoln-castle

*Littledean Jail Museum*, Littledean, nr Cinderford, Royal Forest of Dean,
Gloucestershire GL14 3NL. Telephone: 01594 826659.
Website: www.littledeanjail.com

*The London Dungeon*, 28–34 Tooley Street, London, SE1 2SZ.
Telephone: 0207 4037221. Website: www.the-dungeons.co.uk/London

*National Museum of Scotland*, Chambers Street, Edinburgh, EH1 1JF.
Telephone: 03001 236789.
Website: www.nms.ac.uk/our_museums/national_museum.aspx

*Norwich Castle Museum*, Castle Hill, Norwich, NR1 3JU.
Telephone: 01603 493625.
Website: www.museums.norfolk.gov.uk/Visit_Us/Norwich_Castle

*Ruthin Gaol*, 46 Clwyd Street, LL15 1HP. Telephone: 01824 708281.
Website: www.denbighshire.gov.uk/en-gb/DNAP-7PUFPD

*Tolbooth Museum*, Castle Street, Aberdeen, AB11 5BQ.
Telephone: 01224 621167.
Website: www.aboutaberdeen.com/tolbooth.php

*The Tower of London*, London, EC3N 4AB. Telephone: 08444 827777
Website: www.hrp.org.uk/TowerofLondon

*Warwick Castle Dungeon*, Warwick Castle, Warwick CV34 4QU.
Telephone: 01926 495421. Website: www.warwick-castle.com/explore-castle/the-castle-dungeon.aspx

*The York Dungeon*, 12 Clifford Street, York, YO1 9RD.
Telephone: 01904 632599. Website www.the-dungeons.co.uk/York

# INDEX

56